DISCOVER CALIFORNIA

Redwood National Park

Selected Short Outings

AN AMERICAN TRAVELER SERIES PUBLICATION

by Eric J. Adams

© 1993, revised 2009

This book or any parts thereof may not be reproduced in any manner whatsoever without written permission of the publisher.

ISBN-13: 978-1-55838-153-7
ISBN-10: 1-55838-153-8

American Traveler Press
A Division of Primer Publishers
5738 North Central Avenue
Phoenix, Arizona 85012
www.AmericanTravelerPress.com
1-800-521-9221

Cover Photo of San Diego Bay courtesy San Diego Convention & Visitors Bureau

10 9 8 7 6 5 4 3 2
Printed in China. Published in the United States of America

Redwood National Park

WELCOME

From the mist-shrouded coast of Big Sur to the barren deserts of the Colorado River basin, California travelers can find pristine beauty, and natural surprises, as well as man-made delights.

Take the Pacific Coast Highway. A drive along the cliffs and breathtaking vistas of Highway One reveals a coast remarkably unspoiled. The same is true of the Gold Country, where travelers can pan for illusive treasure under the shade of twinkling Aspen trees.

In the Redwood Country, nature takes a sharp turn upward with Sequoia and Redwood trees that scrape the skies like downtown buildings. Those whose quest is for heights should visit Mount Whitney, the highest point in the contiguous United States at 14,494 feet. Travelers seeking the other extreme can travel 90 miles to Death Valley, the lowest point in the United States at 282 feet below sea level. At Lake Tahoe, it's possible to slip a quarter in a Nevada-side slot machine, then travel five minutes to a California trout hole that you'd swear had never been fished before.

For urban adventurers, California is a delight. Romantic San Francisco, the aquatic pleasures of San Diego, and the stars of Hollywood, all make it apparent that there are many Californias, each a remarkable place waiting to be explored.

Other guidebooks in the California Traveler Series:

A Traveler's Guide to California's Beaches
Earthquake Country Traveling California's Fault Lines
Ghost Towns of California Remnants of the Mining Days
A Guide to California's Historic Sites & Museums
California Missions a Guide to the State's Spanish Heritage
Parks & Monuments of California a Scenic Guide
Railroads of California Seeing the State by Rail
Overnight in San Francisco Enjoying a Short Visit
Whale Watching & Tidepools a Guide to Marine Life

Contents

Welcome	2
Taste The Napa Valley	4
Relax In Sonoma Valley	5
Fun On The Russian River	6
Watch The Whales	7
Dwarfed By Big Trees	8
Highway One North	9
Stand Next To A Volcano At Lassen	10
The Untamed Trinity Alps	11
Tahoe: The Lake In The Sky	12
The Mother Lode	14
Experience Unique Yosemite	15
The Big Trees	16
Boating On Lake Oroville	17
Sacramento: A Capital Time	18
Fresno County's Blossom Trail	19
Golden Gate Park	20
Santa Cruz's Boardwalk	21
Walk The Earthquake Trail	22
San Francisco Magic	23
Map	24
Lock Yourself In At Alcatraz	26
San Francisco's Steepest	27
Death Valley Wildflowers	28
Take A Tram Above Palm Springs	29
The Praying Arms Of The Joshua Tree	30
Surf's Up On The South Central Coast	31
Roam The Hearst Castle	32
The Remarkable Big Sur	33
Tour Monterey Bay & 17 Mile Drive	34
Take The Scenic Drive Around Santa Barbara	35
Movie Making In Los Angeles	36
Cruise To Catalina Island	37
Curves Of The Santa Monica Mountains	38
Historic Long Beach	39
Explore Tinsel Town	40
Tidepools At Cabrillo National Monument	41
Kiss A Whale In San Diego	42
South Of The Border	43
Go To The Beach	44
Footsteps Of The Padres	45
Names & Numbers	46

Wine World Estates   BERINGER VINEYARD

TASTE THE NAPA VALLEY

Ask a Californian to point you to Wine Country and invariably you'll end up in the Napa Valley. This slender 30-mile valley, 50 minutes northeast of San Francisco, is home to some of the world's greatest vineyards, among them Beringer, Franciscan, Hess, Laird, Mondavi and Sterling.

From San Francisco take the Golden Gate Bridge north. Turn east on Highway 37, then north again on Highway 29. From Napa travel north through the charming towns of Yountville, Oakville, Rutherford, and St. Helena until you reach the jewel of Napa Valley, Calistoga. This area has several health spas with hot mineral springs and volcanic ash mud baths. Enroute, stop to sample the seemingly endless varieties of white and red wines. Some wineries charge a nominal fee.

To explore the quieter side of Napa Valley, take Silverado Trail, which runs parallel to Highway 29. The views are nicer and the wineries less crowded. There is a spectacular geyser in Calistoga. Travelers can also rent bicycles in Napa and Calistoga to explore the many side roads, where wineries are located in converted Victorian homes. Several companies offer hot air balloon rides and a variety of companies offer plane, helicopter, or glider rides in the valley. Another conveyance available is the historic Napa Valley Wine Train.

Sonoma Valley Visitors Bureau   HACIENDA WINERY

RELAX IN SONOMA VALLEY

Just west and parallel to Napa Valley lies the lush Sonoma Valley, called by Native Americans "The Valley of the Moon." This is a premiere wine growing region with wines that some say rival Napa Valley's production. Although it has many wineries, Sonoma offers a less crowded wine experience. Sonoma Valley is also home to California's most northerly mission, and is the adult home of Jack London, author of *Call of the Wild*, and *The Sea Wolf*.

For a relaxing day trip by car from San Francisco, take Highway 101 north to Highway 37, then Highways 121 and 12 into the heart of Sonoma. Sonoma Plaza is an old town square, dating to the days when California was Mexican territory. Here, 150 years ago, settlers raised the Bear Flag and declared California's independence from Mexican rule. Today, Sonoma Plaza is the site of many events and festivals throughout the year.

While in the town of Sonoma, detour onto Old Winery Road to two hidden but spectacular wineries, Hacienda and Buena Vista, good stops for a picnic lunch. Continuing on Highway 12, follow signs for Glen Ellen and Jack London State Historical Park. The charming towns of Glen Ellen and neighboring Kenwood are home to more distinguished wineries, including Chateau St. Jean and Glen Ellen. For an overnight stay, Sonoma offers a variety of bed & breakfasts, inns, lodges, and hotels. To return to San Francisco, retrace the route or continue on Highway 12 to Santa Rosa, then down Highway 101.

D. Parker   ALONG THE RIVER

FUN ON THE RUSSIAN RIVER

When a beautiful river meets a beautiful ocean, the results are spectacular. At the town of Jenner, the wide mouth of the Russian River meets the Pacific Ocean. Here each evening, travelers gather to watch the sun set over this magnificent site.

Jenner is just one delight along the Russian River. The area also offers mighty redwood trees, wineries, swimming, boating, fishing and more.

To reach the area, travel up Highway One to Jenner and turn east on Highway 116; or take Highway 101 north from San Francisco to River Road, just north of Santa Rosa.

The lazy Russian River is perfect for recreational canoeing. Forestville and Guerneville have boat rental facilities. For travelers seeking a hot afternoon swim, Memorial Beach in Healdsburg and Johnson's Beach in Guerneville both offer large dammed-off swimming areas, complete with wading spots for kids and offshore floats for experienced swimmers. There are also paddle boats, inner tubes, and canoes for rent.

Hikers can trek under some of the state's tallest coastal redwoods, including the 310-foot Parson Jones Tree in Armstrong Redwoods State Natural Reserve near Guerneville. Bird watchers should keep an eye out for rare spotted owls. The best fishing along the river is in the fall when the silver and Chinook salmon begin their spawning runs. While here, don't miss the famous Korbel Champagne vineyard for a tour on the art of champagne making and a sampling of fine champagne and wines.

California Office of Tourism   DIVING GRAY

WATCH THE WHALES

It's easy to understand what attracts artists and poets to Mendocino, the quaint lumber and fishing village 120 miles north of San Francisco on Highway One. Rugged terrain and Cape Cod-style houses make this an inspiring region.

Passing through the coastal waters nearby are the 40-ton California Gray whales. The best time to watch these majestic mammals is between December and March as they migrate south from their summer quarters in the Arctic Ocean and Bering Sea to warmer waters near Baja California. This 6,000-mile trip takes the whales three months, and no fewer than 10,000 of them make the annual pilgrimage.

California Grays travel in groups called pods, consisting of three to five individuals. Since the whales are usually found ¼ to ½ mile off shore, travelers need binoculars to catch a glimpse from land. Prime observation spots are Laguna Point at MacKerricher State Park and the Mendocino Headlands. For a closer glimpse of these magnificent creatures, take a whale watching excursion from Noyo Harbor at Fort Bragg.

Don't leave town without stopping by the Mendocino Coast Botanical Gardens or the curious "pygmy forest" in Van Damme State Park, where vegetation is dwarfed due to unique soil conditions. Here, full-grown pine trees stand one foot tall. To reach Mendocino from San Francisco, travel north on Highway 101, then head west on Highway 128 or 20 to the coast.

National Park Service   REDWOODS NATIONAL PARK

DWARFED BY BIG TREES

California travelers can easily spend a day or a week under the canopy of the tallest trees in the world. From San Francisco, the nearest place to catch a glimpse of the giant redwoods is in Muir Woods National Monument, just off Highway One, 30 minutes north of the Golden Gate Bridge. The coastal redwood belt runs about 500 miles, much of it along Highway 101, and varies in width from 1 to 20 miles. The best tree specimens are found in Del Norte, Humboldt, and Mendocino Counties.

The Avenue of the Giants begins in Phillipsville, 250 miles north of San Francisco. From here, travelers can wind through 43,000 acres of Humboldt Redwoods State Park, or stop along the way to drive *through* a redwood at one of three commercially-run sites.

For tree watching at its best, visit the 106,000-acre Redwoods National Park between Crescent City and Eureka. A shuttle bus service departing from the information center in Orick takes visitors to Tall Trees Grove. The notoriety of a record-setting 367-foot tree in this grove helped establish the park. However, as tops break off and new growth pushes up, this record fluctuates. Coast redwoods live an average of six centuries with a few living over 2000 years. The park includes more than 120 miles of trails through huge redwood groves that blend into areas of oak woodlands and coastal ecosystems. Hardcore tree lovers can travel north again to Del Norte Coast Redwoods and Jedediah Smith Redwoods State Parks.

National Park Service   GREAT BEACH

HIGHWAY ONE NORTH

No trip to California is complete without a visit to at least one portion of Highway One, the winding, spectacular, and in some places tortuous road that hugs most of the California coast from Oregon to Mexico.

Some of the most rugged and unspoiled coastline can be found north of the Golden Gate Bridge, starting with Great Beach at the Point Reyes National Seashore, just north of San Francisco (pg. 22). For 200 miles, the road twists and turns, traversing the high cliffs and sudden valleys.

Stop at Bodega Bay for a cup of clam chowder and see why Alfred Hitchcock chose this town to film *The Birds*. Gualala and Point Arena are also favorite getaway towns for San Franciscans. While swimming is ill-advised along much of the rocky coast, there are several state beaches as well as unmarked beaches along the way. A small parking lot jammed with cars is usually evidence of a trail leading to a secluded beach.

Travelers should not expect much in the way of amenities on this ride. But the sleepy coastal towns do offer cozy bed and breakfast inns and restaurants serving crab, oysters, clams, and other delights of the sea. At Rockport, Highway One turns inland for more than 100 miles. But along a local road, visitors can explore the rugged "lost coast" from South Fork to Petrolia and Capetown.

National Park Service — LASSEN PEAK

STAND NEXT TO A VOLCANO AT LASSEN

Even though Lassen Peak is an active volcano, the last time it erupted was in 1917. In fact, it erupted 300 times between 1914 and 1917! Despite the volcano's recent dormancy, visitors to the park can still see boiling lakes, bubbling mud pots, hot springs, and cinder cones.

Located 50 miles east of Redding on Highway 44, Lassen Volcanic National Park is completely surrounded by the much larger Lassen National Forest, an area of unparalleled beauty and scores of mountain lakes.

Because of its volcanic activity, the area offers some interesting geologic curiosities. Subway Cave, for instance, is a ⅓-mile tube of hardened lava. Bring a flashlight and jacket for the self-guided tour. Spatter Cone Trail is a 1½-mile self-guided walk through an eerie volcanic landscape. Hat Creek Rim is a 14-mile-long escarpment created when the earth ripped along a fault and was thrust up on one side.

Avid hikers, mountain bicyclists, and horseback riders should travel the Bizz Johnson Trail, a 26-mile saunter along an old railroad logging grade between Susanville and Westwood. The trail snakes through the rugged Susan River Canyon and surrounding mountains. In winter, the area is a wonderland for cross-country skiing and snowshoeing enthusiasts.

Trinity County Chamber of Commerce   TRINITY ALPS

THE UNTAMED TRINITY ALPS

Sprawling northern California is a massive, untouched expanse of mountains, lakes and rivers. It is largely uninhabited, making it a great place to explore the untamed outdoors. Redding, on Interstate Highway 5, three hours north of Sacramento, is the natural anchor to this wild area. From here travelers can easily access three nearby lakes created by the Central Valley Project. All three are perfect for sailing, canoeing, camping, and fishing.

Whiskey Lake, smallest of the three, is just west of Shasta, a town now preserved as a State Historic Park. Take a quick car ride to the town of Hayfork on Highway 3 for a look at the Natural Bridge, a 200-foot arch across a narrow canyon in the Shasta-Trinity National Forest. Northwest is Trinity Lake, the areas second largest lake.

Shasta Lake, the largest man-made lake in California, was created by the impressive Shasta Dam, with a spillway three times as high as Niagara Falls. Snow-capped Mount Shasta looms behind the lake's 370 miles of shoreline. Several marinas rent boats for a day or week. Nearby Shasta Caverns are accessible by diesel-powered catamaran. The ferry service operates year round from its harbor, 20 minutes north of Redding on Interstate Highway 5.

Eagle Lake, just north of Weaverville, is long, narrow and less frequented but just as spectacular as its nearby cousins. For an awe-inspiring drive through the Salmon-Trinity Alps Wilderness to Arcata on the Pacific coast, take Highway 299 from Redding.

TAHOE: THE LAKE IN THE SKY

Even though a portion of the lake lies in Nevada, Lake Tahoe is California's jewel. At 6,229 feet above sea level, it is cradled in the granite setting of the High Sierra, 98 miles northeast of Sacramento.

Many travelers are amazed at the clarity of the deep, blue water. The lake's average depth is 989 feet—1645 feet being its deepest point—and the water is over 95% pure. With a surface area of 193 square miles, the lake holds enough water to cover the entire state of California 14 inches-deep. The lake never freezes over because of its depth and summer water temperatures are cool even on the warmest days. Back from the shoreline much of the adjacent area is National Forest. All around is scenery to frame summer and winter sports in abundance.

A tour around Lake Tahoe makes a great day trip. Use Interstate 80 to get to Truckee, an old west town once famous for lawlessness and saloons. From Truckee take California Route 287 south to Kings Beach for your first view of the lake at Agate Bay. Kings Beach is a center for sailing, water-skiing, rafting, and kayaking. Local marinas here and around the lake rent boats and offer lake tours.

East on Nevada Route 28 will soon bring you to Incline Village on Crystal Bay. Named for the Great Incline Tramway built by loggers in 1878 the term incline is well applied to the area. Some of the planet's wealthiest people have built their mountain retreats on the inclines. Proceeding south on 28, the Highway offers sweeping views of the lake.

Zephyr Cove is homeport for the MS Dixie II a 570-passenger paddlewheeler. A few miles farther south at Stateline take US Highway 50 to South Lake Tahoe and you're back in California. The Tahoe Queen, another paddlewheeler, is berthed at South Lake Tahoe. Both of the paddlewheelers have daily sightseeing cruises. Also at South Lake Tahoe is The Gondola At Heavenly with 138 eight-passenger cabins ready to lift you 2.4 miles over Heavenly Valley for scenic views of Lake Tahoe and Carson Valley. Plan on at least two hours for both the cruise and gondola ride. You can combine lunch with either one.

At Tahoe Valley leave Highway 50 and go north on California State Route 89. You'll stay on 89 until you leave the Lake Tahoe area and connect with Interstate 80 completing your loop. Next stop, if this is a summer adventure, should be the U.S. Forest Service Visitor Center between Camp Richardson and Emerald Bay. Take advantage of the walking trail and be sure to experience the Stream Profile

Lake Tahoe Visitors Authority   FANNETTE ISLAND

Chamber that provides an underground cross-section view of Taylor Creek.

Next on your itinerary is what every tour of Lake Tahoe must include: Emerald Bay, a National Natural Landmark. The Bay itself is an underwater state park, the entire shoreline is within Emerald Bay State Park. In the bay and part of the park is Fannette Island. Crowned with a stone tea house, Fannette is Lake Tahoe's only island. Also in the Park is Vikingsholm, a 38-room granite castle, built in the style of a Norse fortress. There is no automobile access to the shoreline, bring your walking shoes to be rewarded with a view of the bay, the island and the castle.

North of Emerald Bay, D. L. Bliss State Park and Sugar Pine Point State Park are where you want to visit for swimming, camping, nature trails, picnicking, fishing, cycling or cross country skiing. In Sugar Pine Point State Park are examples of a Queen Anne-style summer mansion built in 1902 and an 1870 summer cabin.

Leave the lakeshore at Tahoe City. North of Tahoe City still on Route 89 you'll intersect Squaw Valley Road. The Squaw Valley Cable Car operates year-round and gives an aerial view of the 1960 Winter Olympic Site and Lake Tahoe. Up top are year-round activities, the winter recreation is still Olympic quality. North of Squaw Valley, the road parallels the Truckee River until you reach Interstate 80.

All around the lake, there's plenty to do for the culturally inclined. On the north and south shores of the lake are festivals, and special events, including rodeos, air shows, art shows, craft fairs, farmers markets, jazz concerts, and an annual Shakespeare Festival. Leaf peepers can get a great look at the fall colors from roadside or a hot-air balloon.

Grass Valley and Nevada County CC   PANNING FOR GOLD

THE MOTHER LODE

In the early days, gold could be found by turning over rocks in a riverbed and plucking out the nuggets. Modern travelers to the region's many streams and seven major rivers can still search for flakes of glitter. Gold Country is a 200-mile stretch of Sierra foothills, extending from Grass Valley and Nevada City in the north to Oakhurst and Raymond in the south. Highway 49 traverses the entire route and is appropriately called "The Gold Chain." Oakhurst, with its false front buildings, stone courthouses, and Gold Rush museums, is typical of the Old West towns along the highway.

Next travel north through Mariposa and Colterville. Well-preserved Jamestown is where such movies as *High Noon* and *Butch Cassidy and the Sundance Kid* were filmed. Railtown 1897 State Historic Park, near the edge of town, contains the rolling stock of the Sierra Railroad. Columbia, two miles past Sonora off Highway 49, also has been restored as a state historic park, vintage 1860s.

Farther north is Angels Camp, the locale for Mark Twain's *Celebrated Jumping Frog of Calaveras County*. The towns of San Andreas, Jackson, Sutter Creek, and Diamond Springs offer more Gold Rush thrills. Historic Nevada City, developed as an inland retreat for wealthy families from San Francisco, offers horse-drawn carriage rides, an Art Deco courthouse, and several bed and breakfast inns. Grass Valley is home to Empire Mine State Historic Park, site of the oldest, richest, hardrock gold mine in California. In operation from 1850 until 1956, an estimated 5.8 million ounces of gold were extracted from 367 miles of underground passages.

National Park Service   YOSEMITE VALLEY

EXPERIENCE UNIQUE YOSEMITE

Teddy Roosevelt called it the most beautiful place on earth, and most visitors to Yosemite agree. The park boasts 200 miles of primary roads and 750 miles of trails. Popular Yosemite Valley accounts for only 1% of the park's 1,170 square miles, but is home to many waterfalls and such legendary formations as Half Dome and El Capitan.

Other sites offer beauty all their own. Glacier Point, accessible from Highway 41, offers an overlook with a commanding view of Yosemite Valley. For sweeping views of the Sierra, take Tioga Pass Road, a 39-mile drive that crosses Tuolumne (TWAL-o-me) Meadows, the largest sub-alpine meadow in the Sierra.

The Mariposa Grove of Giant Sequoias is located 36 miles south of Yosemite Valley via Highway 41. Activities include hiking and ranger-led walks to one of the world's oldest and largest sequoias, the Grizzly Giant. Also in Mariposa Grove is the California Tree, a walk-through tunnel tree.

Summer traffic is heavy at Yosemite, but the park provides complimentary shuttle bus service. Yosemite Valley offers more than 1,200 rooms, cabins, and tent cabins; reservations are a must. A wilderness permit is required for overnight stays in Yosemite's back country. In winter, Badger Pass Ski Area, the oldest in California, offers beginner and intermediate skiing, as well as 90 miles of cross-country trails.

National Park Service　　　　　　　SEQUOIA PARK

THE BIG TREES

Sequoia National Park is one of the few places on earth where, in a span of 45 miles, travelers can ascend from 1,700 feet to 14,494 feet. Along with adjacent Kings Canyon National Park, Sequoia offers much of the beauty of Yosemite with a fraction of the crowds.

Accessible via State Route 180 from Fresno or 198 from Visalia, the two parks range from the brushy foothills of the San Joaquin Valley to the barren peak of Mount Whitney, highest point in the contiguous United States. The 46-mile General's Highway is the primary road that connects the two parks. More than 1,000 miles of trails cut through a magnificent display of sequoia groves, granite mountains, and glacial lakes.

Sequoia is home to 4 of the world's 5 largest sequoia trees, including one called General Sherman. At 102.6 feet girth and 274 feet in height, it is reputed to be the largest tree on earth. The General Grant, in Kings Canyon National Park's Grant Grove, is a few feet thicker but not as tall.

The Congress Trail Loop, an easy 2-mile hike, winds past groups of Sequoias. At Tunnel Log, travelers can drive under a fallen giant. Crystal Cave shelters unusual geological formations, and breathtaking Moro Rock offers a 360 degree view of the Sierra and surrounding valleys.

Lake Oroville District — SYCAMORE COVE

BOATING ON LAKE OROVILLE

Just a few miles from the City of Oroville is Lake Oroville State Recreation Area, one of the premier boating lakes in the state. Man-made Lake Oroville is located on the Feather River, where California's central valley meets the Sierra foothills. The area is about an hour's drive from Sacramento on State Route 70, then east on 162.

It is the lake's shape—a spidery mass of crooked forks—that makes it a mariner's delight. With 167 miles of shoreline, boaters can explore hidden coves and canyons while enjoying warm temperatures and the distant vistas of Plumas National Forest. Lime Saddle and Bidwell Canyon Marinas rent boats. In the spring, mariners can travel within a quarter mile of 640-foot Feather Falls.

The Feather River Fish Hatchery, located below the dam on Table Mountain Blvd., is open for tours. It's particularly delightful during autumn when the salmon and steelhead run. Special windows give visitors a unique view of fish leaping their way up the ladder to the hatchery. The lake is a mecca for anglers since it is stocked annually with trout, bass, catfish and salmon.

Hikers can enjoy the Feather Falls Hiking Trail, a moderate 3.5-mile walk to an observation platform overlooking Feather Falls. The Oroville Dam, 770 feet high and 3,000 feet thick at its base, is the highest earth-filled dam in the United States. An exhibit at the visitor center tells the story of the dam's construction.

Dave Henry, Sacramento CVB   RIVERBOAT DELTA KING

SACRAMENTO: A CAPITAL TIME

Ninety minutes northeast of San Francisco, Sacramento is a river town built on the confluence of the American and Sacramento Rivers. Both provide hundreds of miles of waterways for fishing, swimming, and rafting in the lazy style of Huck Finn. Travelers can view several replica paddle-wheel river boats permanently docked in town, a testament to the days when Sacramento was a bustling supply center for Gold Rush prospectors. For a self-guided tour of Sacramento's earliest settlement, visit Sutter's Fort at 27th and L Streets.

The Sacramento Zoo houses more than 700 animals in open-air grottoes, islands, and other natural settings. It is located in William Land Park, which also includes a large playground, picnic area, golf course, fairy-tale town, and sports facilities. Old Sacramento is a 28-acre National Historic Landmark with more than 100 restored and re-created buildings from the 19th century. Railroad buffs should visit the California State Railroad Museum, largest of its kind, at the corner of 2nd and I Streets. For old car fans, there's the Towe Auto Museum on Front Street., home to the most complete collection of antique Fords in the world.

The Crocker Art Museum, oldest public art museum in the west, boasts a fine collection of European paintings. The Victorian Governor's Mansion, former home to California's governors and now a State Historic Park, is now a museum of 19th century culture.

Demi DeSoto — BLOSSOM TRAIL

Fresno County's Blossom Trail

California's central valley is to agriculture what Hollywood is to entertainment. Rich soil combined with irrigation in the San Joaquin Valley has produced one of the nation's premier agricultural districts. Cotton, grapes, oranges, and turkeys are the headliners. Tour some of the finest stone fruit orchards in the region by driving the Blossom Trail.

With the Sierra Nevada as a backdrop, travelers can catch the Blossom Trail at Ashland Avenue in Fresno. Follow the pink and blue "Blossom Trail" signs around the 62-mile full-circle tour.

While the drive is always scenic, it is especially beautiful in the early spring, when the pink, red, and white blossoms of almond, apricot, citrus, plum, peach, and apple trees appear. Traveling east on Highway 180 offers a view of the tall mountains of Sequoia and Kings Canyon National Parks. Turning south, the Trail, brings travelers to the community of Reedley. The beautiful Kings River flows through the town, there are opportunities for boating, fishing, rafting and swimming. Take a few moments to visit the Mennonite Quilting Center to experience seeing handmade rug and quilt making plus gaze at the grandest mansions in Fresno County and visit the Reedley Opera House.

Continuing through some of Fresno County's million-plus agricultural acres, notice many of the tree trunks are painted white. This helps prevent scorching of trees by the hot sun. The full circle tour can be completed in two to six hours depending on stops.

San Francisco CVB　　　　　　　　TEA GARDEN

GOLDEN GATE PARK

Once a wasteland of shifting sand dunes, Golden Gate Park is one of today's preeminent urban parks in the world. Stretching more than 30 city blocks, the park is home to museums, arboretums, gardens, and a number of hiking and biking trails.

The thousand-acre park is located between Baker Street on the east and the Pacific Ocean on the west. The big cultural attractions are the California Academy of Sciences, M.H. de Young Museum, the Japanese Tea Garden, the Conservatory of Flowers and the Strybing Arboretum. Travelers can buy a single pass to the sites, all within walking distance of each other.

There are at least two dozen recreational opportunities in the park, including a golf course, tennis courts and lawn bowling. Boat and bicycle rentals are available at Stow Lake and there's also an exquisitely restored working carousel at Children's Playground. Riding lessons are offered at the Golden Gate Park Stables. Bike and roller skate rentals are available at a number of shops along Lincoln and Stanyan Streets.

The best way to see the park is on foot or bicycle. Start at the Music Concourse. Travel west through the many foot trails to Stow Lake and on to the Buffalo Paddock near 36th Avenue for a look at a bison herd.

Santa Cruz County Conference & Visitors Council   BOARDWALK

SANTA CRUZ'S BOARDWALK

Before the likes of Disneyland and Universal Studios, there were good old-fashioned amusement parks like the one in Santa Cruz. California's only operating beach front amusement park, the Beach Boardwalk is a cornerstone of Santa Cruz history and culture.

The classic 1911 carousel and the Giant Dipper roller coaster are National Historic Landmarks. Other attractions include more than 25 rides, a vast old-time arcade, shops, and restaurants. The park is adjacent to the beach, so sunbathing is an additional option.

Santa Cruz, located at the northern tip of Monterey Bay, is hugged by redwood forested mountains. It's the epitome of the California beach community, with sun-drenched surfers and bikini-clad sun bathers. Another Santa Cruz must is a ride on The Roaring Camp and Big Trees Railroad. The historic narrow gauge train leaves from the Wharf for the 2-hour journey through the magnificent San Lorenzo River Canyon.

For more Santa Cruz fun, try the Mystery Spot on North Branciforte Drive. Here, where the laws of gravity appear to be reversed, balls roll uphill and visitors find themselves leaning at precarious angles.

The Municipal Wharf on Beach Street is a hot spot for pier fishing. Enjoy a meal, then stroll along the pier and watch the sea lions, pelicans, and passing boats. Deep sea fishing trips, excursions, and bay cruises depart regularly from the Wharf.

National Park Service   POINT REYES LIGHTHOUSE

WALK THE EARTHQUAKE TRAIL

Travelers crossing into Point Reyes National Seashore, just 35 minutes north of San Francisco, are also crossing over the San Andreas Fault—from one major tectonic plate to another. San Francisco, along with most of the United States, is on the North American plate. Point Reyes is on the very eastern edge of the Pacific plate. The slow movement of the two plates in opposite directions is the cause of earthquake activity in the Bay Area.

Whether it's the result of geology or some other force, Point Reyes is a place of rare beauty and fragility. The Bear Valley Visitors Center, just off Highway One near Olema, was the epicenter of the great 1906 earthquake. This is a good spot to begin the tour. The Earthquake Trail is a .7-mile walk (also wheelchair accessible) along the San Andreas Fault. It's one of several self-guided tours that highlight everything from earthquake geology, to estuary life, to the migration patterns of the gray whales.

From Bear Valley, turn left on Limantour Road, 8 miles to Limantour Beach, a good spot to wade, watch birds, beach comb, or picnic. The lighthouse at the very tip of Point Reyes offers a fantastic view of the Pacific. On a clear day, travelers can see the distant Farallon Islands. Inland Tomales Bay gives another view of ocean life. Marshall Beach, a short walk from the parking lot, is a great place for children to swim, since there are calmer waters on the bay side of the park.

San Francisco Convention & Visitors Bureau CABLE CARS

SAN FRANCISCO MAGIC

Travelers with only one day to visit San Francisco should see the 49-square-mile-city via its famous 49-Mile Scenic Drive. This tour doesn't cover all of San Francisco, but it takes in the major historic, and cultural attractions as well as a taste of some of its cozy neighborhoods famous scenery.

The planned route is well marked by blue and white sea gull-emblazoned signs. Begin any place along the drive; a good spot is the city's Civic Center at Van Ness and Hayes. The drive goes through Japantown, the posh shopping district of Union Square, colorful Chinatown, and chic Nob Hill. Stop on Telegraph Hill and take public transit to Coit Tower for one of the city's best views. Those who like gift shops and seals should stop either at Pier 39 or Fisherman's Wharf.

The 49-mile drive bypasses crooked Lombard Street, but a detour onto Russian Hill will rejoin the drive near Fort Mason where it runs along San Francisco's famed Marina district.

Next, it's down to the beaches and the zoo, up through Golden Gate Park, and on to the top of Twin Peaks, one of the highest points in San Francisco. Continue to Mission Dolores for a taste of the city's Hispanic neighborhood. This drive, with stops, takes the entire day and shows the best San Francisco has to offer.

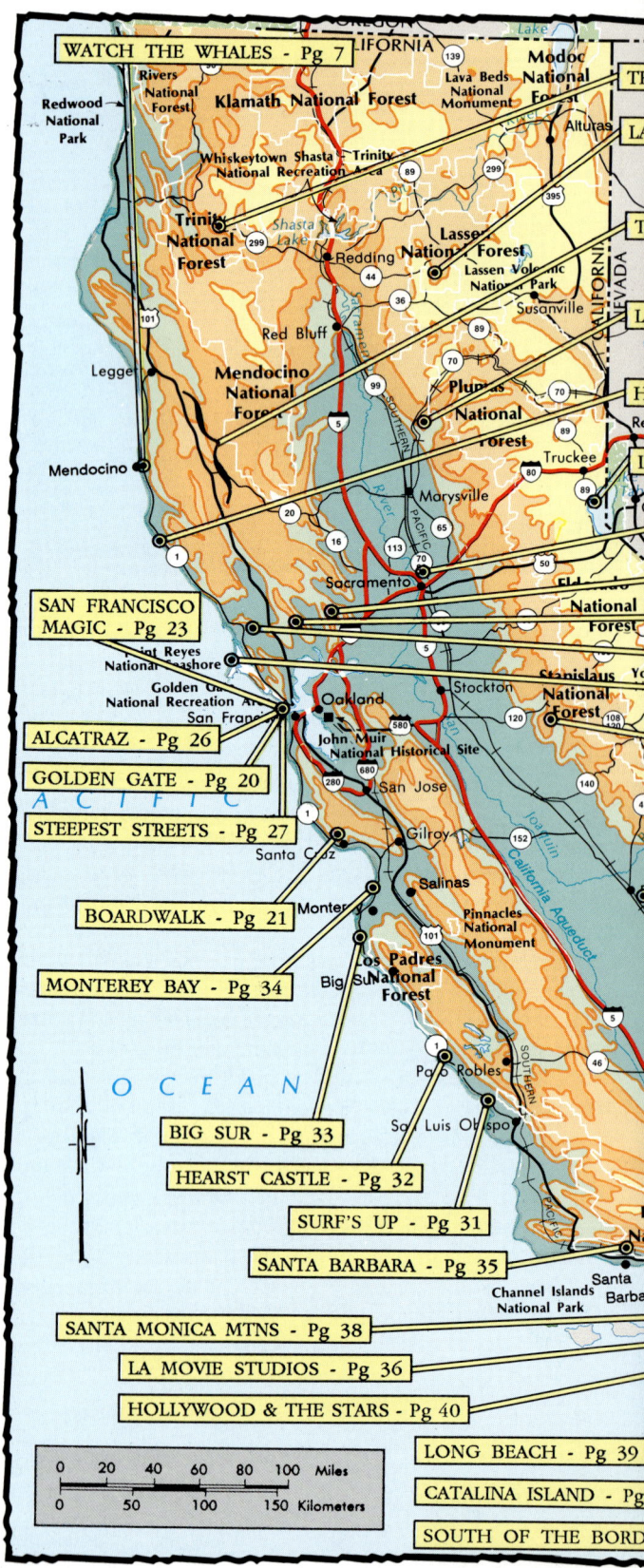

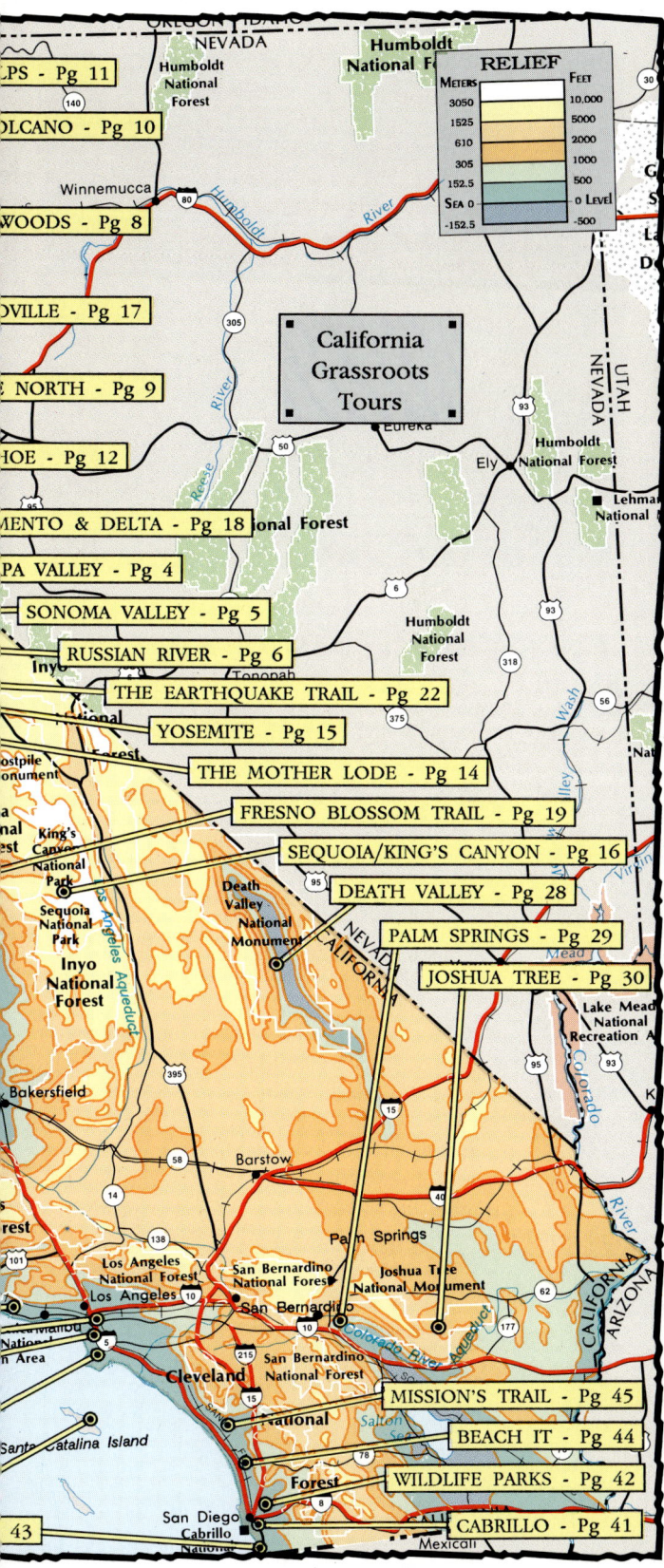

California Office of Tourism ALCATRAZ

LOCK YOURSELF IN AT ALCATRAZ

One of the highlights of a trip to San Francisco is the ferry ride to one of its most famous landmarks, Alcatraz Island. Once the prison home of such notorious criminals as Al Capone and The Bird Man of Alcatraz, the federal prison, known as *The Rock,* has been closed since 1963.

Today Alcatraz is part of the Bay Area's 74,000-acre Golden Gate National Recreation Area. Access to the 12-acre island is free, but there is a ferry fee. The Red & White Fleet boats cast off at 30-to 45-minute intervals from Pier 41 at Fisherman's Wharf. Reservations are highly recommended.

On the island, travelers can take a tour of the main prison block with its steel bars, claustrophobic 9 × 5-foot cells, mess hall, library, and "dark holes" where inmates were sent for solitary confinement. Tour guides will be happy to close one of the steel-plated doors behind any unruly visitor, to dramatize the sense of complete isolation. Also the site of California's first lighthouse, mariners and tourists still benefit from its light.

The island offers great views of the Golden Gate Bridge, nearby Angel Island, and San Francisco, 1-¼ miles away. Those who listen closely will hear, as the prisoners did, the laughter of the revelers on Fisherman's Wharf.

San Francisco CVB A STEEP ONE

SAN FRANCISCO'S STEEPEST

When you're traveling the streets of San Francisco and encounter a traffic sign that reads "Hill," believe it. San Francisco has 42 hills and at least two are traversed by streets with a gradient greater than 30%. (In comparison, a steep mountain pass has a 7% grade). Ready for some adventure? Here is San Francisco's top ten list!

		Grade
1.	Filbert between Leavenworth and Hyde	31.5%
2.	22nd Street between Church and Vicksburg	31.5%
3.	Jones between Union and Filbert	29.0%
4.	Duboce between Buena Vista and Alpine	27.9%
5.	Jones between Green and Union	26.0%
6.	Webster between Vallejo and Broadway	26.0%
7.	Duboce between Divisadero and Alpine	25.0%
8.	Duboce between Castro and Divisadero	25.0%
9.	Jones between Pine and California	24.8%
10.	Fillmore between Vallejo and Broadway	24.0%

Rules of the road: go slowly, pump your brakes, keep your eyes open.

Don't miss Lombard Street., billed as the most crooked street in the world, with 9 hairpin turns in a single block. There's an old saying about the City by the Bay, "When you get tired of walking around San Francisco, you can always lean against it."

National Park Service — DANTE'S VIEW

DEATH VALLEY WILDFLOWERS

Think it gets hot in Death Valley? Look at some of its place names: Stovepipe Wells, Furnace Creek, Dante's View, Badwater Basin. Yet if the fall and winter rains are plentiful, a blanket of spring wildflowers will cover the huge desert park annually. There are more than 900 plant species here. February to June is the best time to catch the colorful show of Desert Bear Poppy, Cacti, Mariposa Lily, Lupine, Mojave Wildrose, Paintbrush, and Mojave Desert Rue, to name a few.

Death Valley National Park hugs California's border with Nevada, approximately 150 miles northwest of Las Vegas and 300 miles northeast of Los Angeles. Precipitation is sparse, with an average annual rainfall of only 1.9 inches. Summertime temperatures can reach 120–125 degrees.

In addition to the flowers, travelers will find a magnificent array of other flora, fauna, wildlife, and geologic formations. Badwater on the valley floor, 282 feet below sea level, is the lowest spot in the Western Hemisphere, yet it is within 90 miles of Mount Whitney (14,495 feet), the highest point in the contiguous United States.

Many features in the Park can be reached by car from the Furnace Creek Visitor Center. Here, travelers can choose a number of 1- to 4-hour drives to places like Natural Bridge, a relic of an ancient waterfall, or Artists Drive, a 9-mile route through the color-splashed Black Mountains, or the intriguing man-made Scotty's Castle off Highway 267.

Palm Springs Aerial Tramway   THE TRAM

TAKE A TRAM ABOVE PALM SPRINGS

Palm Springs, "America's Desert Playground," is known for its celebrity residents, superb golf courses, and sunny, hot weather. Located 107 miles east of Los Angeles, the city of Rolls Royces and swimming pools boasts 354 days of sunshine.

One of the best ways to see this desert oasis is from the Palm Springs Aerial Tramway. A dramatic ride on Swiss-style cable cars takes travelers from the desert floor to a mountain station 8,516 feet above sea level in Mount San Jacinto State Park.

The tram, departs at half hour intervals during daylight hours year-round. The ride covers 12,800 feet with a vertical ascent of 5,873 feet—more than a mile. The two 80-passenger enclosed cars travel on 11 cables weighing 330 tons.

Up top is a gift shop and observation area, as well as 54 miles of hiking trails, five campgrounds, and the Nordic Ski Center, open in winter. The highlights of the trip are views of Palm Springs and the desert that stretch for 75 miles. Naturalist John Muir described the view as "the most sublime spectacle to be found anywhere". To reach the ride from Palm Springs take Highway 111 to Tramway Road.

National Park Service   JOSHUA TREE NATIONAL PARK

THE PRAYING ARMS OF THE JOSHUA TREE

The poetically named Joshua Tree is actually a giant member of the agave family, attaining heights of 30 feet. It got its name, the story goes, from the up stretched branches, that reminded Mormon pioneers of Joshua beckoning people to the promised land.

The Joshua Tree symbolizes the beauty and richness of the Mojave Desert that stretches from Palmdale, just north and east of Los Angeles, into Nevada. Joshua Tree National Park is approximately 50 miles northeast of Palm Springs. There are park entrances on both Highway 62 and Interstate 10.

With altitudes ranging from 1,000 to 6,000 feet the park supports a diversity of plants and wildlife. The Joshua Tree Forest is just part of the reward for birdwatchers and wildflower enthusiasts. The mighty Joshua trees grow at the higher elevations in the central and western parts of the park.

Take a self-guided nature tour to a palm oasis from Park Headquarters in Twentynine Palms, or a car trip to the large boulders of Hidden Valley, once said to have been a hideaway for cattle rustlers and other rogues of the West. Contemporary residents of Hidden Valley include Desert Bighorn Sheep. For sweeping vistas of both mountains and deserts, visit Keys View, a side trip off the main park route south of Hidden Valley.

Monterey Visitor & Convention Bureau   ALONG HIGHWAY ONE

SURF'S UP ON THE SOUTH CENTRAL COAST

California's sea-sculpted coast from San Simeon to Ventura, a 200-mile drive, includes picturesque towns and some of the state's finest beaches. At the northern edge of this region is Morro Bay, where shoreline cottages are decorated with seashells and driftwood. Nearby Morro Bay State Park offers a Museum of Natural History.

Traveling south, San Luis Obispo is 12 miles inland. Here Highway One is also signed as El Camino Real. San Luis Obispo is a good place to get the feel of a mission town, the mission was built in 1772. Travel nine miles south again and your back on the coastline near Pismo State Beach home of the largest over-wintering colony of monarch butterflies in the United States.

At this point Highway One again travels inland for a lengthy course through Lompoc and on to Gaviota State Park before again skirting the coast. Now, Refugio State Beach and El Capitan State Beach are your windows to Channel Islands National Park just a few miles off-shore.

University of California at Santa Barbara is just north of the city, Santa Barbara itself is a separate and rewarding tour. Ten miles south near Carpinteria, is the next best thing to the North Pole. Santa Claus Lane is a block-long stretch of gift shops, all featuring Christmas themes. Finally it's on to Ventura to visit San Buenaventura Mission on East Main Street or stretch out on the coastal beaches where the water is decidedly warmer than in the north.

Hearst Monument/John Blades   FROM THE AIR

ROAM THE HEARST CASTLE

There is nothing quite like the lavish, legendary estate of publishing magnate, William Randolph Hearst. La Cuesta Encantada® is tucked in the Santa Lucia Mountains, overlooking the Pacific Ocean and Highway One. Today, Hearst San Simeon State Historic Monument gives you accessibility to Hearst Castle®. It took craftsmen nearly 30 years to create the mansion and guesthouses; construct the pools and walkways; cultivate the acres of gardens and terraces.

La Casa Grande is the name given to the main house. It has sitting rooms, a billiard room, theatre, library, guest suites, a kitchen larger than most homes, and a wine cellar with rare European vintages as well as California wines. Hearst's vast art collection is displayed throughout the castle. In addition, the estate includes indoor and outdoor pools, tennis courts, and three guesthouses.

The guesthouses are named Casa Del Monte, Casa Del Sol and Casa Del Mar. The smallest with a modest 10 rooms is Casa Del Monte and Casa Del Sol has 18 rooms. Casa Del Mar is the largest and most elaborate of the guesthouses. The three are separated by elaborate gardens, terraces and walkways accented with marble sculptures.

The buildings and grounds are so extensive that four separate tours with very little overlap are needed to see them all. Each tour takes about 2 hours and covers one area of the estate. One of the tours requires climbing up and down over 400 stairs, the others require fewer stairs and there is a no-stair version of one of the tours. In addition to day tours, evening tours are sometimes available. Reservations are recommended.

Monterey Visitor & Convention Center   BIG SUR

THE REMARKABLE BIG SUR

For a 90-mile stretch between Carmel in the north and Sam Simeon in the south, Highway One roams through one of the most spectacular stretches of scenery in the world—Big Sur. Flanked by the Santa Lucia Mountains and the rocky Pacific coast, the Big Sur is not a destination tourist attraction. Most of the Big Sur area is protected from development by Los Padres National Forest so there are no large towns or villages, no golf courses or shopping malls, and few permanent residents. But there are plenty of high cliffs and grassy promontories dotted with wildflowers.

While amenities are few but not absent, Pfeiffer Big Sur State Park, Garrapata State Park, and Andrew Molera State Park offer camping, swimming, hiking and fishing opportunities. Pfeiffer Big Sur State Park has a lodge and conference center.

With a good pair of binoculars, travelers can sight the California gray whales as they pass by during their yearly migrations. The offshore area has been declared a refuge for California sea otters, which live contentedly on the abundant kelp beds. Harbor Seals and Sea Lions are also residents of the area. Bird watchers should keep a lookout for the California brown pelican, the red-billed oystercatcher, golden eagles, owls, valley quail, and belted kingfishers.

Monterey Bay Aquarium　　　　　　　　　　THE AQUARIUM

TOUR MONTEREY BAY & 17 MILE DRIVE

The cypress-covered Monterey Peninsula is crowded with natural and cultural wonders from its southern edge in chic Carmel-by-the-Sea to the town of Monterey, site of the famous Monterey Bay Aquarium. Carmel is at the southern entrance of the renowned 17-Mile Drive.

This toll route takes travelers past some of the world's most spectacular seascapes, palatial estates, world-class golf courses including Pebble Beach, Spanish Bay and Spyglass plus the natural beauty of the Del Monte Forest. At the northern end of the drive is Pacific Grove, Butterfly Capital of the World. Each autumn millions of orange and black monarch butterflies migrate here, as well as other sites in the region, to spend the winter.

Under the flags of Spain, Mexico and the United States, Monterey was the capital of California. Today, Monterey is a bustling tourist port with Fisherman's Wharf and the famous Cannery Row, immortalized by John Steinbeck when the region was the sardine capital of the world. At Cannery Row travelers can visit the spectacular Monterey Bay Aquarium, offering a fascinating look at the undersea landscape of the Bay, one of the richest marine environments in the world. The aquarium is home to more than 6,500 sea creatures including the popular sea otters. Among the other area attractions is the Maritime Museum of Monterey. Located in Monterey's historic Custom House Plaza, the museum features priceless and unique artifacts and exhibits relating to the region's maritime history.

Santa Barbara Convention & Visitors Bureau   THE COUNTY COURTHOUSE

TAKE THE SCENIC DRIVE AROUND SANTA BARBARA

There are two ways to tour this year-round resort town of soap opera fame. The Red Tile Walking Tour is a 12-block journey through the city's charming downtown. The 15-mile Scenic Drive (maps available in town) gives travelers a sweeping tour of greater Santa Barbara.

The Scenic Drive starts at the illustrious courthouse on Anacapa Street. Climb the 85-foot clocktower for a panoramic view. Next is El Cuartel-El Presidio de Santa Barbara, the Historical Museum, and The El Paseo—an Old Spanish-style shopping arcade. At the nearby Santa Barbara Museum of Art, travelers can view of the works of O'Keefe, Hopper, Chagall, Pisarro and others. The Museum of Natural History houses the giant skeleton of a blue whale and exhibits on prehistoric Indian life.

Mission Santa Barbara with its twin bell towers is a Catholic parish church open to the public year round. Santa Barbara's Botanic Gardens are devoted entirely to the study of California's native flora. The city also has a superb zoo. Nearby Stearns Wharf is the oldest operating wharf on the west coast.

For the architecturally-minded, this tour includes two historic homes, the 14-room Victorian Fernald House and the Trussel-Winchester Adobe, built with adobe bricks, timber, and brass from a wrecked ship. The finale, at Yacht Harbor and the Hope Ranch Residential Area, shows travelers why Santa Barbara residents would never dream of leaving.

Universal Studios   UNIVERSAL STUDIOS

MOVIE MAKING IN LOS ANGELES

For an inside view of Los Angeles' legendary entertainment industry in action, take a day-long excursion through the back lots and special effects stages of Universal Studios, Warner Brothers Studios, or Paramount Pictures.

Universal Studios, the world's largest television and motion picture facility, is located in Universal City, right off Highway 101. The Metro Line Subway can also take you there. The box office is open daily but best to reserve tickets ahead of time. The tour includes a narrated tram ride through acres of famous movie and television sets.

Warner Brothers Studios on Hollywood Way in Burbank is less glitzy than Universal. Guides lead 10 to 12 persons through sound stages, a $20-million wardrobe inventory, back lot streets and the Warner Brothers Museum that always has charming exhibits. The 2-hour tour leaves twice daily.

Tours at Paramount Pictures on Melrose Avenue in Hollywood are on a first come basis. Arrive early at the visitor center on Gower Street for the 2-hour weekday tour of the daily operations of Paramount's picture and television facility. You may be able to squeeze the Warner and Paramount tours into one day, but leave an entire day to experience the extravaganza of Universal Studios.

Santa Catalina Island Company   AVALON BAY

CRUISE TO CATALINA ISLAND

Few automobiles are allowed on beautiful Catalina Island, 26 miles across the sea from Long Beach and San Pedro harbors. But public transportation is available for a number of tours of island highlights. Travelers will find sandy beaches, clear blue waters, and hidden harbors reminiscent of the Mediterranean.

Five cruise companies provide frequent daily departures to the island from Long Beach, San Pedro, and Newport Beach, which take 1 to 2 hours, depending on the point of departure. San Diego and Oceanside take 3 to 4 hours.

Once in Avalon, the island's main port, travelers can stroll through the charming town or investigate water sports. Visitors can jet ski, paddle board, kayak, parasail, scuba dive, snorkel, and swim. Glass bottom boat and semi-submersible submarine tours of a nearby cove, known as the "undersea garden," provide a magnificent display of marine plant life and colorful fish. A nature conservancy and the Wrigley Memorial and Botanical Garden are showplaces for native island plants.

The island's Art Deco casino, made famous during the 1930s and 1940s, once attracted the biggest names in Hollywood and the Big Bands of the era. The tour includes the Avalon theatre with its rare pipe organ, and the Casino ballroom, a 180-foot circular dance pavilion with no interior columns.

California Office of Tourism   SANTA MONICA MOUNTAINS

CURVES OF THE SANTA MONICA MOUNTAINS

The beach town of Malibu is famous as a Hollywood hideaway and a mecca for tanned surfers. But it is also gateway to the Santa Monica mountains, a patchwork of state, federal, and private parks, reserves, and ranches that offers incomparable views of the ocean, mountain scenery, and some exhilarating driving experiences.

The Santa Monica Mountains are accessible from Highway 101, but the most scenic entry is from Highway One. Just east of Malibu, enter Topanga Canyon on Topanga Canyon Boulevard. At the intersection with Old Topanga Canyon stay left and take Old Topanga Canyon Road. The road winds its way up the mountain with a series of narrow, hairpin turns. At the top is the famous Mulholland Highway. Go left and follow this scenic corridor west along the spine of the mountains for some 50 miles.

The drive offers city panoramas of the San Fernando Valley and the Los Angeles Basin, as well as sweeping vistas of the ocean. There are plenty of well marked vista points to stop at in the mountains. A number of north/south roads, such as Malibu Canyon Road and Kanan Road will take travelers from Mulholland back to Highway One with many good beach stops along the way. If time permits, it is well worth following Mulholland Highway to its terminus at Carrillo State Beach, 28 miles northwest of Santa Monica on Highway One.

Long Beach Area CVC   SHORELINE VILLAGE

HISTORIC LONG BEACH

California's fifth largest city is a favorite embarkation point for boaters and fisherman as well as one of the Pacific Coast's busiest shipping centers. Land-lovers can also view some diverse architecture here. The Ocean Center Building on West Ocean Boulevard is an example of Mediterranean Revival; its octagonal tower is a hallmark of the city's skyline. On East Ocean, the elaborate ornamentation of the Breakers Hotel is Spanish Revival and the triple-gabled Pacific Coast Club is reminiscent of a French manor house. Built in 1906, the First National Bank Building on Pine Avenue is an example of French Renaissance style, the clock tower is a long-time landmark.

   The Long Beach Convention and Entertainment Center on Ocean at Long Beach Boulevard is adjacent to the Aquarium of the Pacific and Shoreline Village. The Center hosts trade shows, concerts, plays and sporting events. The Aquarium's Research Vessel Tour provides an excellent view of the downtown shoreline and adjacent Los Angeles Harbor as well as the opportunity to view marine life. Shoreline Village offers shops and boat rentals but its premiere attractions are Lion's Lighthouse and the 1906 carousel.

   Another Long Beach gem to include in your tour is the Queen Mary. The ocean liner is permanently docked in the Harbor and is a floating hotel and restaurant. Moored next to Queen Mary is the Russian submarine Scorpion. Tours of both ships are open daily.

Los Angeles CVB　　　　　　　　　　　　　　　　HOLLYWOOD

EXPLORE TINSEL TOWN

Hollywood's first motion picture studio was established in 1911. There are just as many ways to see Tinsel Town as there are legends about it. Most sightseeing tours will give you a glimpse of celebrity homes.

Don't miss Grauman's Chinese Theatre on Hollywood Boulevard. For a look at the hand and foot prints of Hollywood's legends, as well as imprints of Betty Grable's leg, Jimmy Durante's nose, Donald Duck's webbed feet and John Wayne's fist. The Walk of Fame extends along the Boulevard and then south on Vine. Just down the street is the Egyptian Theater, Grauman's first movie palace and site of Hollywood's first movie premiere. At the Hollywood Wax Museum also on the Boulevard, travelers can see replicas of their favorite stars.

The Capitol Records Tower, at the famous corner of Hollywood and Vine is designed to look like a stack of records topped with a stylus. The light at the building's top blinks Hollywood in Morse Code. John Lennon's Walk of Fame Star is in front of the tower. There are three recording studios in the building but no public access is provided for.

In the foothills is Hollywood Bowl, a natural amphitheater that hosts the Los Angeles Philharmonic Orchestra and a variety of other presentations mostly musical. Adjacent is the Edmund D. Edelman Hollywood Bowl Museum. The Hollywood Bowl Hall of Fame and interactive musical wall for children make the museum and grounds a worthwhile stop even without a concert.

THE OLD LIGHTHOUSE

TIDEPOOLS AT CABRILLO NATIONAL MONUMENT

Cabrillo National Monument, at the southern tip of Point Loma in San Diego, is one of the smaller national monuments but don't let its size fool you. The monument is home to a teeming city of tidepool life.

On the western side of the park, where the ocean meets the land, is a rocky environment of marine plants and animals that have adapted to harsh tidal conditions. Here are the flowery anemone, the scavenging shore crab, grazing limpets, spongy dead man's fingers, and hundreds more species that look strangely unfamiliar. The glassed-in observatory at the monument is a great place to view the Pacific gray whale migration in winter.

For a casual hike, try the Bayside Trail. Along it is a unique example of a coastal chaparral forest, as well as remnants of a coastal artillery system built to defend San Diego harbor during World Wars I and II. Another landmark is the old Point Loma lighthouse, the beacon that welcomed sailors to San Diego Bay from 1855 to 1891.

To reach the monument, take Rosecrans Street (Highway 209) south. Turn right on Canon Street and left onto Catalina Boulevard. Catalina will provide spectacular views of the city and ocean enroute to the Monument.

Sea World of California — SHARK TANK

KISS A WHALE IN SAN DIEGO

San Diego is home to three world-class wildlife parks, any of them a full-day trip. Sea World on Mission Bay is a wonderland of aquariums, exhibits, and shows. But the undisputed draw is the killer whale team of Shamu and Baby Shamu. The pair performs daily before delighted (and wet) crowds. Here, too, travelers can see the world's largest collection of live sharks, 350 penguins, and a walrus pool. Sea World is but one attraction on the 4,600-acre Mission Bay, a multi-island playground of beaches, boat-launching ramps, picnic areas, campgrounds, playgrounds, and golf courses.

The world-renowned San Diego Zoo is in Balboa Park, the heart of San Diego. The zoo is home to more than 4,000 animals including Sumatran orangutans and Chinese leopards. This zoo was one of the first in the world to replace cages with habitats that closely resemble the natural environment of the resident.

Thirty five miles north in Escondido is San Diego Zoo's Wild Animal Park. Over 3,000 animals from more than 250 species roam the 1,800-acre park. Many plants and animals native to Africa and Asia thrive in the San Diego climate. Hop the Skyfari Aerial Tram for a bird's-eye journey into the wild, or walk along Kilimanjaro Safari Walk or Elephant Overlook. To reach the Wild Animal Park, travel north on I-15 to the Via Rancho Parkway exit.

Bob Yarbrough — TIJUANA MARKET

SOUTH OF THE BORDER

A popular trip from San Diego is the short jaunt across the border into Mexico. Tijuana, the first stop, is Mexico's most-visited city. Attempts to clean up the city's tawdry image have been only partially successful, but there is an unmistakable energy in Tijuana.

Travelers can shop for inexpensive Mexican gifts and handiwork, visit the Agua Caliente Racetrack on evenings and weekends, or see a bull fight during the summer. There's no need to convert American currency; dollars are happily accepted, but travelers should bring small bills.

Rather than drive to Tijuana, take the San Diego Trolley from downtown to the border, or walk across the border and catch a cab to the downtown section. Travelers who do drive should pick up a short-term insurance policy at the border, since most American insurance policies are invalid in Mexico.

The city-weary traveler can avoid border towns altogether by driving 70 miles south on Highway One to Ensenada, a resort town and sport fishing center on Todos Santos Bay. This laid-back town, the port of call for several cruise ships, boasts fine restaurants and shops. Estero Beach south of town is a favorite among swimmers and surfers.

To the south is Baja, an 850-mile stretch of desert and mountains. The roads aren't always in good repair, but travelers are rewarded with fantastic beaches as well as lovely towns and vistas.

City of Oceanside OCEANSIDE PIER

GO TO THE BEACH

Along Highway One from north of San Diego to Oceanside is a delightful string of sandy beaches, charming towns, and sweeping vistas, worthy of both cameras and swim suits. Start in the fashionable enclave of La Jolla, 15 minutes north of San Diego. Prospect is the main street in town, with rows of art galleries, boutiques, restaurants, and small hotels.

Drive 10 minutes up North Torrey Pines Road to a wind-swept 1,750-acre preserve of gnarled torrey pine trees, one of only two places where these trees grow. Walk along the marked paths among the preserve's cliffs and canyons, then down to 6 miles of gorgeous beaches. Just up the highway is the town of Del Mar, a mecca for thoroughbred racing fans during the summer. Del Mar offers more boutiques and galleries. Ballooning is a favorite activity, and several companies offer hot air flights.

The two towns of Encinitas and Leucadia afford more picturesque southern California vistas. Flower lovers can visit 30 acres of rare plants at Quail Botanical Gardens, east of Encinitas Boulevard. Carlsbad, another 10 minutes north, is known for its Old World architecture. Though the spring is inactive, the town is dotted with small hotels and spa facilities. Oceanside, the last city before the Camp Pendleton Marine base, has a 1900-foot pier, a favorite among fisherman. The restaurant at the end of the pier is a good place to watch the many races and regattas that take place here.

City of Oceanside   MISSION SAN LUIS REY

FOOTSTEPS OF THE PADRES

Three of the most magnificent missions in California are located near San Diego: San Diego de Alcala, San Luis Rey, and San Juan Capistrano. Missions were central to the Catholic church's attempt to convert native Americans and colonize California. Whether the attempt was successful is hotly debated. But the beautiful missions are reminders of California's colorful, turbulent, past.

San Diego de Alcala was the first mission dedicated in what is now California. Founded by Father Serra in 1769, the mission was moved to its present site in 1774. Because it was the first of the California missions, it has been designated a basilica.

Mission San Luis Rey de Francia is one of only four missions still owned by the Franciscans, the loyal order that spearheaded the mission crusade up the California coast. Dubbed "King of the Missions," San Luis Rey once included 6 acres of buildings and supported 3,000 native Americans. The town is 5 miles east of Oceanside off California Highway 76.

Visiting San Juan Capistrano on March 19 gives travelers an opportunity to witness the famous and inspiring return of the swallows from their southern winter feeding grounds. This "Jewel of the Missions" was destroyed in the earthquake of 1812. Travelers can visit the Serra chapel and view the elaborate masonry of the Great Stone Church, now in partial ruins. Take Ortega Highway exit west from I-5 in San Juan Capistrano.

Tahoe North VCB   LAKE TAHOE SKIERS

NAMES & NUMBERS

BIG SUR CHAMBER of COMMERCE
Big Sur, CA 93920
(831) 667-2100
www.bigsurcalifornia.org/

CABRILLO NATIONAL MONUMENT
San Diego, CA 92106
(619) 557-5450
www.nps.gov/cabr/

CALIFORNIA DEPARTMENT of PARKS & RECREATION
Sacramento, CA 95814
(800) 777-0369
www.parks.ca.gov/

CATALINA ISLAND CHAMBER of COMMERCE
Avalon, CA 90704|
(310) 510-1520
www.catalinachamber.com/

DEATH VALLEY CHAMBER of COMMERCE
Shoshone, CA 92384
(760) 852-4524
www.deathvalleychamber.org/

EUREKA CHAMBER of COMMERCE
Eureka, CA 95501
(707) 442-3738
www.eurekachamber.com/

FRESNO CHAMBER of COMMERCE
Fresno, CA 93716
(559) 495-4800
www.fresnochamber.com/

GOLDEN GATE NATIONAL PARKS
San Francisco, CA 94123
(415) 666-7200
www.nps.gov/goga/

GRASS VALLEY CHAMBER of COMMERCE
Grass Valley, CA 95945
(530) 273-4667
www.grassvalleychamber.com/

HEALDSBURG CHAMBER of COMMERCE
Healdsburg, CA 95448
(707) 433-6935
www.healdsburg.com/

HEARST CASTLE
Hearst San Simeon State Historical Monument
(800) 444-4445
www.hearstcastle.com/

JOSHUA TREE NATIONAL PARK
Twentynine Palms, CA 92277
(760) 367-5500
www.nps.gov/jotr/

LAKE OROVILLE STATE RECREATION AREA
Oroville, CA 95966
(530) 538-2219
www.parks.ca.gov/?page_id=462

LAKE TAHOE
North Shore (800) TAHOE4U
South Shore (800) AT TAHOE
www.laketahoechambers.com/

Redwood National Park

LASSEN VOLCANIC NATIONAL PARK
Mineral, CA 96063
(530) 595-4444
www.nps.gov/lavo/

LASSEN NATIONAL FOREST
Susanville, CA 96130
(530) 257-2595
www.fs.fed.us/r5/lassen/

LONG BEACH CHAMBER of COMMERCE
Long Beach, CA 90831
(562) 436-1251
www.lbchamber.com/

LOS ANGELES CHAMBER of COMMERCE
Los Angeles, CA 90017
(213) 580-7500
www.lachamber.com/

MALIBU CHAMBER of COMMERCE
Malibu, CA 90265
(310) 456-9025
www.malibu.org/

MENDOCINO COAST CHAMBER of COMMERCE
Fort Bragg, CA 95437
(707) 961-6300
www.mendocinocoast.com/

MONTEREY PENINSULA CHAMBER of COMMERCE
Monterey, CA 93940
(831) 648-5360
www.mpcc.com/

NAPA VALLEY CONFERENCE & VISITORS BUREAU
Napa, California 94559
(707) 226-7459
www.napavalley.org

NEVADA COUNTY CHAMBER of COMMERCE
Grass Valley, CA 95945
(800) 655-4667
www.grassvalleychamber.com/

PALM SPRINGS CHAMBER of COMMERCE
Palm Springs, CA 92262
(760) 325-1577
www.pschamber.org/

PARAMOUNT STUDIO TOUR
Hollywood, CA 90038
(323) 956-1777
www.paramount.com/

POINT REYES NATIONAL SEASHORE
Point Reyes Station, CA 94956
(415) 464-5100
www.nps.gov/pore/

REDDING CHAMBER of COMMERCE
Redding, CA 96001
(530) 225-4433
www.reddingchamber.com/

Redwood National Park

REDWOOD NATIONAL & STATE PARKS
Crescent City, CA 95531
(707) 464-6101
www.nps.gov/redw/

SACRAMENTO VISITORS BUREAU
Sacramento, CA 95814
(916) 808-7777
www.sacramentocvb.org/

SAN DIEGO VISITORS BUREAU
San Diego, CA 92101
(619) 232-3101
www.sandiego.org/nav/Visitors

SAN FRANCISCO VISITORS BUREAU
San Francisco, CA 94102
(415) 391-2000
www.sfcvb.org/

SAN LUIS OBISPO CHAMBER of COMMERCE
San Luis Obispo, CA 93401
(805) 781-2777
www.visitslo.com/

SANTA BARBARA VISITORS BUREAU
Santa Barbara, CA 93101
(805) 966-9222
www.santabarbaraca.com/

SANTA CRUZ COUNTY VISITORS BUREAU
Santa Cruz, CA 95060
(831) 425-1234
www.santacruz.org/

SANTA ROSA CHAMBER of COMMERCE
Santa Rosa, CA 95404
(707) 545-1414
www.SantaRosaChamber.com

SEQUOIA NATIONAL PARK
Three Rivers, CA 93271
(559) 565-3341
www.nps.gov/seki/

SONOMA VALLEY VISITORS BUREAU
Sonoma, CA 95476
(707) 996-1090
www.sonomavalley.com

UNIVERSAL STUDIOS
Universal City, CA 91608
(800) UNIVERSAL
www.universalstudioshollywood.com/

WARNER BROTHERS STUDIOS
Burbank, CA 91522
(818)954-3000
www2.warnerbros.com/wbsf/

YOSEMITE NATIONAL PARK
Yosemite, CA 95389
(209) 372-0200
www.nps.gov/yose/